Love Ya Later, Bye

By Kimberly Tayman

Copyright © 2018 Kimberly Tayman

All rights reserved. No part of this publication may be reproduced, distributed, or transmitted in any form or by any means, including photocopying, recording, or other electronic or mechanical methods, without the prior written permission of the publisher, except in the case of brief quotations embodied in critical reviews and certain other noncommercial uses permitted by copyright law.

Dedication

For you, Mom.

Love ya later, bye.

Preface

Several years ago, following the death of my mother, I decided that I would write a book to memorialize Mom's life, utilizing her doodles and the 148 cassette tapes I recorded over the phone during her terminal illness, to help paint a complete picture.

The first three years I had the tapes, I could not bring myself to look at them, let alone listen to them. I would write down stories that I could remember and keep them in a folder, hoping one day to bring them all together in a collection.

This went on for several more years. I would write a little here, a little there, but never seriously sat down and worked on my project. Eventually, I was ready to try listening to the tapes, so I pulled one out and put it in my tape recorder for playback. I only made it through one side of the very first tape, but I did it. I couldn't bear to listen to any more, so the tapes sat for yet another year.

It was about this time that I realized it would only take one small disaster to destroy my recordings, and they would be lost forever. I had to digitize them for safekeeping, which meant I was finally forced to listen to them all. I transcribed some of the tapes, but still had not made any real progress on my book.

On August 24th, 2017, I realized that I only had 12 months until my mother would have been gone a full decade. This gave me the impetus to finally finish the task I had assigned myself. I gave myself a one-year deadline to complete the book for the occasion.

Over the last year, I have written…a bit. I found that listening to the recordings was still more of a painful experience than I had anticipated, so I tended to avoid the task.

Lo and behold, a month prior to my deadline, I realized that if I didn't kick it into gear, I would not meet my self-imposed target. That's when I began writing in earnest. Any and all errors, mistakes or lapses of memory are entirely my own, I mean I didn't give my editor much time to work.

In true Kimberly fashion, I waited until the last minute. I had procrastinated so long, and I was terribly naïve about the difficulty of publishing a book. But I refused to give up. Therefore, I now present to you a raw and unpolished look of what I learned about Mom, as well as myself.

Acknowledgements

My heartfelt thanks to:

Booknook.biz for helping me format on the fly.

My extended family and friends, who endured endless calls and incessant questions to help me understand Mom better.

My helpful "first draft staff" Kelly Samuelson, Kimmie Doss, Justin Hefner, Marquita Parkan and Michelle Jennings, for the help with typos and blaring mistakes.

My dad for being the best Dad a girl could ask for.

Garrhett and Makenna Kidd, for making me the "cool" aunt.

My sisters, Tracy Kidd and Mackenzie Miller, for trusting me to tell moms story. Carmine and Tiger would be so proud of you.

Susan, Michael, and Olivia Biay for allowing me to have my three greatest joys in life: being a mom, a mother-in-law mom and a Mona. Susan especially for telling me to go for it with no regrets.

My husband, Craig, for loving me when I didn't

love myself. For showing me that I can use my evil impulses for good purposes. For making this book a priority even when he didn't have the time. For helping me find my writing style and trying to edit this hot mess in just two short weeks. ILYAHAW

Hello, Wonderful!

My mom was born Linda Susan Feeback on April 24, 1951, in Versailles Kentucky. She was a cute, brown-eyed, curly-haired bundle of joy for my grandparents. Grandpa William was a decorated war hero and Grandma Margaret Feeback (Teater) was a fashionista and a battle-tested "domestic General." They came home to a pretty, modest, white house surrounded by beautiful, thick trees and acres of deep, green grass on Sugar Creek Pike Road. I imagine that as a child, she was surrounded with love and affection from her extended family, most of whom lived nearby.

She was the oldest of eight kids, the longest gap between them being three years, which happened to be Mom and her brother, Willie. After Willie came Debbie, Robin, Jorja, Kay, Larry, and the baby, Carl. Except for a two year pause every now and then, infants were coming one right after the other. Oh, man, I feel for my grandma and her lady-parts.

Shortly after Mom turned three, the family began to move around, due to Grampa's job in the Army. I believe she never really felt planted anywhere, or that any one location was "home." Her childhood was typical of the age, consisting mostly of her assisting with the care of her siblings. She was in her mid-teens when she endured her last move with her family, to Fort Leonard Wood, Missouri. It was at this base that she met my dad.

My dad, Mack, was born to Miller and Grace (Smith) Upchurch on July 23, 1946 in Caruthersville Missouri. He was an above-average looking kid, and his good looks carried on into his older years. He was one of six children and as he says, they "had a simple life." Usually, his schedule consisted of waking up to help with household chores before going to school. On the weekends, he and his brothers, sometimes his sisters as well, would help pick cotton, plow the fields, and buck hay barrels on neighbors' farms. Dad said this was the essence of his life, day in and day out, until he was drafted in 1966 at the age of 20. He went to Basic Training at Fort Leonard Wood, and snagged an assignment there directly after training. By this point, he considered himself a well-travelled man, at least compared to his family, who had never left their town before. Just one short year later, he encountered my mother.

Dad was a strong-jawed private with a buzzcut

when he met Mom at the Soto Service Recreation Center on base, where he was working.

It's funny how family folklore has a way of evolving stories in the telling, like a huge, multi-generational game of telephone. As I remember the story being told to me (which sounds far more romantic to me, and I wish it was the truth), my dad and mom met on a blind date set up by friends. Because of her young age, she was illegally working at the rec center on the base. They connected during the date, fell in love, and married three days later after crossing the state line, because she was only 13.

While writing this book and consulting with my dad for facts, I tried to confirm the story with him to verify everything I remembered. He told me I had lost my ever-loving mind, that he would've *never* married a 13-year-old girl!

"Your mother had just turned 16 and at the time, it was normal to get married so young," he told me, scolding. He continued forcefully, "So, no, Kimberly, I didn't marry your mother at 13, after three days of dating, by crossing state lines in secrecy. In fact, I married your mom after three *months* of seeing her each day at my work. After getting to know her, after falling in love with her. In secrecy? Come on…her mother was our witness!" He went on to chuckle and say, "Don't get me wrong, though, her dad didn't know."

Way to screw up a good tale, Dad.

Shortly after getting married, my dad was sent to Korea and my mom stayed in Fort Leavenworth, Kansas, with her family. After his Korean tour, Dad came home to pick up his wife, and they were off to Germany. That is where my oldest sister, Tracy, was born. She stormed into my parents' lives in November of 1971 at the 97th General U.S. Army Hospital in Frankfurt. Mom always said she was the mischievous one. Tracy was constantly getting into situations and was searching for answers about life, even at a young age. She had an insatiable desire to learn, which continued into adulthood. Mom would say that it drove her crazy that her daughter was so smart, but never completed anything. Once Tracy thought she knew enough about one subject, she immediately moved onto the next.

Upon completion of yet another military assignment, my dad, mom, and their little baby returned to the U.S. They came back home to Fort Leonard Wood, Missouri, but this time only for just six months.

Next, they were off to Hawaii, where yours truly came screaming into the world. My grandfather was stationed there, and my dad was lucky enough, or he had enough connections, to be able to bring Mom back together with her family again. I think Dad recognized Mom's melancholy and knew how important it was for her to be near her people. My parents lived the "island life" for three more years before heading to Fort Benning, Georgia.

Fort Benning is where my little sister, Mackenzie, became the final addition to our family. She was born at Martin Army Hospital in April of 1978. "She was a very easy pregnancy," Mom told me. Nothing in life ever seemed to faze her, she wouldn't let much bother her, whether it be falling down and skinning her knee, or being tortured by her older sisters. Mom loved the calmness Mackenzie brought into her life. She was the baby of the family, and Mom loved to spoil her when she could.

But Martin Hospital wasn't only a source of happiness, unfortunately. It was also where my mom's life imploded due to the death of my grandma. Margaret passed away October 1978, just six short months after my mom gave birth. During this stage of life, which should have been blissful, full of baby clothes, midnight feedings and treasuring all her blessings, she was forced to bury her mother. I believe that when she buried her mother, she was also burying her happiness. No one in the family can recall her being glad after that.

Just on the heels of Margaret's death, my dad got orders back to Germany.

This is where my mother seems to have found herself, as well as some small form of happiness.

In Europe, Mom finally came into her own. She found an entry-level job at the military commissary at Robinson Barracks in Stuttgart, Germany. She was able to quickly work her way up to lead cashier, a job she truly enjoyed and, quite frankly, she became the queen of her own little fiefdom.

Germany was a place where she dominated, a place that afforded her the opportunity to branch out and form friendships. Until the day she died, she had her closest friendships with those buddies she met in Germany. Debbie, Wendy, Sally, Kathy, and Sarah remained close to her for the rest of her days. Even though she was not much of a letter-writer, she would comment of her fondness for these true friends and would savor those few reunions when they occurred.

After several extended tours in Germany, nearly eleven years, it was time for my family to return stateside. My dad retired from the Army after 24 years and he and mom moved to Arizona. Her brothers and sisters, save two, were living in the

Phoenix area, where my mom and dad had retired. She would venture out to spend time with them, at least she would when they were on speaking terms. When they were on, they were *on*. We had parties, BBQ's, played softball, went roller skating and to the movies, laughed more than should be allowed and were almost always inappropriate. But when they were *off* they were one Molotov cocktail away from a full-blown riot.

Although she returned to working at the nearest commissary when we moved to Arizona, Williams Air Force Base soon closed, and she had trouble finding work after that.

Normal, day-to-day life carried on. The bills were paid, the house was cleaned, laundry was washed, family was fed. She wasn't always as sad as it may sound. There were plenty of things she loved: people-watching, learning, Pac-Man and Centipede, reading, and she loved her "pretties," meaning her collectible knick-knacks, and found her nirvana in a great casino, with a good cigarette and an ice-cold Coke. And she loved to laugh. She lived her life on her own terms, which meant primarily caring for her girls and her grandchildren.

Mom would often tell me she recalled the first three years of her life, and that she thought they might have been the only time in her life that she was genuinely happy.

How sad that a life lived only 57 years was filled with so little perceived joy?

I would like to think it was only some of her theatrical musing, as she was known to do, but I believe on some level, in some deep-seated philosophy, she meant it when she said, that she felt that lack of happiness, and the depression was her daily reality. I wish I had asked her for more details as to what made her feel this way. During the times we did talk about her overwhelming sadness, she would explain there were moments of happiness in her life, such as when she got married, the birth of her children and grandchildren, and a few other stray memories. But she claimed that mostly she felt deeply cheated in life and those few, happy memories got her through every day.

She worked very hard to help provide for us and rarely did anything for herself. There were four years that she made sure my sisters and I were "dressed to the nines," and she literally only wore the same three outfits for those four years. She never made a fuss about her lack of new clothes or grumbled at our lack of appreciation. I guess she retained enjoyment from seeing her daughters happy and was satisfied. One thing she did insist on, was that we girls always took away some lesson that was learned from our experiences.

You don't realize when you're young what your parents sacrifice for you. For the record, my dad also wore the same outfit for four years also, but it was government-issued, so I guess that's why *he* didn't complain.

It takes great strength to live a life in which one just exists and never realizes true self-actualization. But it is also a sad and depressing life.

I encourage everyone to learn a lesson from Linda, don't just exist, *live*. Recognize that happiness isn't material possessions, but real relationships formed with genuine people.

Lesson learned: *Live* your existence.

Blank Spaces

I know a *lot* of people.

However, I don't really think that people know me. People know me, of course, but I don't think they *know* me. Understand me. The reason I think this is, is because, quite simply, I don't show others who I really am.

Since the age of nine or ten, I've always kept people at arms' length. It wasn't so much a choice as a defense mechanism. Everyone has some sort of inner demon, or a challenging, figurative mountain they are compelled to climb in their lives. My inner demon was created because of a real Demon that lived downstairs from my family's apartment. My mountain manifested when a mountain of a man decided that I would be his play-toy. This nightmare occurred regularly from that time until I was around the age of 12 or 13, as near as I can recall.

When I was a young child, I was a happy girl. I can remember that. What I can't remember is the horrific act that changed who I was. I know the reason, though. It was because of the Demon that lived below me, who changed who I was as a person.

It's difficult for me to remember, because most of my life since that time is filled with black, blank spaces where memories should be. I've had so many good memories and experiences, but I can't fully recall them, because I have this cloud from my past incessantly hanging over me. I don't think that I'm very joyful, to be honest. I've experienced amazing times, wonderful people, and great friends, very few people that know me realize the turmoil I deal with daily. The struggle I always feel, to just *exist*. What it takes to wake up each morning, and dredge through the unhappiness puddle that the Demon left in his wake. How for the first couple hours of each day I must remind myself what a wonderful life I possess.

I stated earlier that the move to Germany allowed Mom to flourish and find herself. Paradoxically, for me, Germany is where I lost myself and my cherished innocence.

I know that I've visited places and have had adventures with my family and friends because I have photographs, but I don't remember the experience…I remember only the image from the photo. It's as if I watch my own life on replay in a video recorder. I know that being sexually abused at such a young age split me in to two different people. I don't mean like some crazy "Sybil," who embodies two distinct, different personalities. But I do have two different personality traits inside of me. One is the person who I show everyone, the happy-go-lucky, cheery woman who is quick to offer help and assistance to others. The other individual shows up when I am safe at home, struggling to fight off a major anxiety attack. Neither one of these personalities are *me*, but I am an amalgam of them both. Over the years memories have faded, have been stitched together differently, but the crux of it all is always the same: what I really am, is *fractured*.

In the process of seeking to help me, my husband has asked me several times how my molestation first happened, how the Demon groomed me, how he made me keep silent about the terrible things he did to me. The truth is that I simply can't remember. I remember an innocent, care-free childhood, then at about the age of nine or ten, I only remember the dread and revulsion of being in this person's presence. That bastard robbed me of my memories.

But in return he taught me much.

The Demon taught me how to lie, because he expected me to do that to my parents. He taught me what guilt meant, he taught me what shame was, all these things that I felt at an age that should have been filled with mere innocence.

He also created a child who was very hard for my parents to comprehend. Although my mom loved me, she couldn't fathom why I was so angry, sad, withdrawn. Why I would hole up in my room for days, not wanting to shower, or to go outside. Why, no matter what she did, even if I smiled on the outside, my eyes were filled with misery.

I begin to use mechanisms for defense. I started eating more, hiding candy and gorging at night. My young 10-year-old brain thought that if I was fat, maybe he would think I was ugly, and not want to do anything to me. That Demon created my persona as the Funny Fat Chick, because although being fat could possibly repel him, it also made me the butt of many childhood jokes, and I used humor to deflect those. I have carried both the weight and the humor into adulthood.

Although I was friendly towards people, I never really had any close friends as a child. I perceived that I was always viewed as an outcast. Even if I wasn't a pariah, in my mind I felt that I was *less than* everyone else, which was then reflected on my exterior. I didn't feel good about myself, so I tried lying to make people like me. To impress my peers, I demanded the best of everything from my parents, and they accommodated me, when they could. I was up-to-date on the latest fashions and I possessed the newest gadgets. I had everything I thought that I needed to make me "cool." The Demon made me feel like I wasn't good enough for anyone, including him. He repeatedly told me that I was a bad girl for letting him molest me, and that now that he had, no one would ever like me if I told them about it.

At about 12- or 13-years-old, I reasoned that if I smelled bad, maybe he would then want nothing to do with me. I wouldn't shower. I didn't brush my teeth. I didn't brush my hair. It got to the point that I started soiling my pants. By this time, I was an adolescent who knew better, but at the same time, I couldn't come up with a better strategy to make his torture stop. I didn't know how to protect my family. The Demon made it clear that if I shared "our secret" with anybody, he would kill my family. How does a young girl even process such a threat as this?

The threat was real to me. He had access to my family. He lived only sixteen short steps from our front door. The Demon was very good friends with my parents. They asked him, and his family, to dinner often. We had barbecues together. He would bring me gifts for Christmas and on my birthday.

The odd thing was that he only brought presents to *me*, never my sisters. I hoped that fact might set off some alarm bells with my family, but unfortunately, it didn't.

It wasn't like this person was on the periphery of my life. He was always around my family, enough to know my parents' schedule, so in my young brain I thought I was protecting my family by saying nothing.

Oddly, my strategy seemed to be working on some level. Mom was somewhat clued-in to what was going on. I was 13 and she was doing my laundry. While she was scrubbing out my filthy pants, she asked me, pleading, "Please, baby, is anyone doing anything to hurt you? Is anyone hurting you, honey? You can tell me, I'll protect you, I promise. Kimmy, even if it's your father, I will protect you!" I wanted to tell her so badly, to let her know that Dad hadn't done these terrible things, that he was in danger too. But how could I risk the safety of my family?

So in the end, I told her nothing.

Soon after that incident, I decided to start taking showers, brushing my teeth, combing my hair, and just otherwise acting "normal." I figured that if I continued to act like a three-year-old when it came to hygiene practices, it would only invite more questions, which would put my family in further danger, so I stopped using my defense mechanisms.

While we lived in Germany, I never uttered a word to Mom. I just saw her pain and how afraid she was and how she felt like she couldn't help me, so I had to act like everything was okay, so she would be okay.

Although my poor sanitation had ceased, I was still a less-than-perfect child. I was angry. Angry about everything. I would lash out at my sisters, my parents, my schoolmates, everyone except the individual who truly deserved my rage. I was still overeating and gaining weight, even though my mother and father thought I was perfectly normal, I was far from ordinary. The anger subsided slightly when the Demon received orders to move to a new duty station. I felt such relief that I had managed to survive the trauma without any harm to my family. Only six more months and I would be free of him forever.

However, the damage that son-of-a-bitch left in his wake would stay with me far into my adulthood and, I would venture to say, even today.

During my teenage years and into early adulthood, I was a horrible person to people. I was mean, I did unkind things, I said cruel things. I threatened to beat people up and manipulated situations for my own advantage. I didn't know how to stop my destructive behavior at this point. I felt as though my bad deeds were a freight train just rolling down the hill picking up speed, and I was tied to the tracks at the bottom of the hill, waiting to be crushed. I became a grade-A, rat-bastard, lying, cheating bully.

I was 16 when we moved back to the States. We had lived in Germany for so long, it was almost as if we were visiting a foreign country, which I guess we were, in a way. I was thrilled to be moving on in my life. Leaving Germany set me free, even if it trapped my mother.

I don't recall whether I was 18 or 19, but my parents received a Christmas card from the Demon. It was one of those cards that had a family portrait on one side. And in the picture, next to the Demon and his wife, was a young girl. His daughter. When I saw that card, I felt a wave of nausea come over me. He now had a plaything of his own, who couldn't get away or escape.

I have decided that I would not mention the Demon's name in this book, nor that of his wife, because that beast of a woman made sure the coast was clear for him every time he violated me. She would walk in, observe what was going on, and the

Demon would order her to go check the windows to ensure no one was approaching. She *knew*. I hold them both culpable. But if I were to expose them here, honestly, I'd be afraid of exposing myself to possible litigation.

But I do think I need to mention the young girl's name. Her name is Stephanie. I feel like I owe her an apology. I often wonder if my silence of his abuse left the door open for that sick *freak* to hurt her. Stephanie, if by some quirk of fate you are reading this, I sincerely and wholeheartedly apologize. I was not strong enough to stop him. If your dad did to you what he did to me, I'm sorry I didn't say anything sooner. I'm sorry I let the statute of limitations run out. I'm sorry I left you at the hands of the Demon. And if you were lucky enough that he only loves you like a father *should* love a daughter, maybe he learned his actions were wrong and stopped. If that's the case, I'm happy for you.

The Christmas card did give me a little bit of information, however. It gave me his last name and his address, but at this point in my life, I didn't know what to do with the data. What I did do was finally admit to my mom what had happened to me. After I was done explaining, she hugged me while tears streamed down her cheeks and apologized for not reading my desperate signs better. When Dad found out, he angrily marched towards his car. He intended to drive to the airport, fly to the Demon's house, and kill him. Mom managed to stop Dad, convincing him that rotting in jail was no way to support a family.

My self-sabotage lingered. My constant need to feel accepted and loved led me to both my greatest challenge, but also my greatest gift, my daughter, Susan.

While I was in high school, a young man showed me attention, which at the time made me happy. Just like a lot of young couples, we felt that we were "in love." But how many 16-year-olds know what love really means? I wasn't equipped to sustain a relationship with myself, let alone someone else. I was still dealing with my inner turmoil, and life was a struggle for me.

After dating a short while, I honestly can't remember how long, I found out I was pregnant. Oh, dear Lord, what had I gotten myself into? I was a high school student with no means to support a baby.

Since my father was retired from the Army, I had insurance, so I was able to receive prenatal care in secret. No one knew I was having a baby until two weeks before Susan arrived.

I came home from school to find my mom standing just inside the door, staring at me.

She was weirding me out, a little. "Hi Mom," I said, tentatively, "what's up?"

"Do you have anything you want to tell me?" she asked, raising an eyebrow.

I froze. "Uhhhh. No. I don't think so?" It was more of a question than a statement.

"Really. Well, your OB/GYN called and had something to tell me. We better get going, they need to see you right away because you have pre-eclampsia, and you need to be monitored."

I'm sure the color drained from my face. I couldn't reply.

Mom heaved a big sigh and continued, "Kim, I'm not happy about this, but we will make sure you and that baby are safe. How long until your due date?"

"Two weeks," I answered, meekly.

"WHAT?!" she yelled. "Are you kidding me? How on Earth did you hide this for so long?!"

I just looked down at my baggy clothes and didn't say anything.

It's almost needless to say that she cycled through every emotion possible in that moment, and in those two weeks that she had left to mentally prepare herself. Naturally, she settled on the feeling of love, and her newest granddaughter, Susan, became the newest star in her world.

Susan was born in November 1993, at Luke Air Force Base's 56th Medical Group Hospital in Arizona. Incidentally, it was the same building where Susan's husband, Michael, now works as a medic today. I think it's so wonderful to know that he leaves the doors every evening that I walked through to bring my baby home.

I believe it was two days after giving birth that I was back to school. No classmates were aware that anything unusual had happened. The first day back, a few friends questioned where I'd been for those days and I simply replied, "I just had a baby."

Stunned silence. Then giggles. "Oh, shut up! You did not!" They didn't believe me until I brought Susan in one day to show everyone.

The young man and I continued our relationship. I knew we were going nowhere and I think he probably knew as much, too. We moved on in life and only communicated about Susan.

After having Susan, I would love to claim that I was a super-mom. That having that beautiful baby magically turned my life around. Unfortunately, that is not even remotely close to the truth. I was still floundering around like a fish out of water. I was gasping for air while everyone else seemed to be excelling in their lives.

I lived with my parents until Susan was two-years-old. Like she always did, Mom managed to take on everyone else's problems as her own. She immediately solved my biggest problem by quitting college to take care of Susan. She was that girl's constant caretaker from the time I went to school until I went to bed.

My mom and dad were picking up all the slack and paying for everything. I did receive some child support, roughly $150 per week, in the beginning. But babies are expensive and there were many extra things that my parents needed to buy. My folks asked me about getting a little bit of money from me to help with the additional bills. When I say a little bit, I mean a pittance. Only $25 per week is all they requested. Nothing unreasonable at all.

I don't know why that angered me, or why I thought, "How dare you?!" I was furious. I couldn't be reasoned with. Logically, I took the next rational step and moved out.

That's right ladies and gentlemen. To avoid giving my wonderful parents a mere $25 per week, I managed to put myself in the hole for $800 per month in rent.

What a genius.

This decision forced me to struggle, working multiple jobs to make ends meet. The entire time, Mom watched Susan, even though she must've been hugely irate with me.

Since the numerous jobs only barely made my life sustainable, I used my feminine wiles to enhance my income. I am not at all proud to admit this, but I felt forced to take advantage of men, exploiting their impulse to "rescue" a woman. To be clear, I was *not* a prostitute. It wasn't like I was doing anything illegal, although if I'm truthful, there were a few things that danced on the razor's edge of morality.

Although my poor ethics and self-sabotage was not completely eradicated yet, I was trying to make myself a better person. I begin to steer my ship a little straighter, and by the time I met my husband, Craig, I was floating along at a steady pace, just slightly off center.

I met Craig on Love@AOL, back when internet dating was still a novelty. He had a profile with a picture that caught my attention, I wrote to him, and our story was off and running. Communication flowed freely. The laughs and jokes we shared started to help me to drop my guard a little. He's a man of solid moral character and just what a screw-up like me needed. His parents did a great job raising a great man.

I was intrigued by this gentle soul, but I was also

reserved with him in the beginning. I was prone to fits of anger and capriciousness, but he must've sensed that I needed him. One night he set me down on the edge of the bed and said, "Something's bothering you, tell me." Even though our relationship was still new, there was a kindness in his eyes that inspired trust. I hesitated for a moment, but he continued, "It's okay, just talk." Oh boy did I talk. I told him every rotten thing I did to anyone. Every lie, cheat, exaggeration, and mistake. After that, the words just tumbled out. I told him about my childhood, and everything that made me into this bitter, hurt woman.

He looked in my eyes, held my hand and said, "But that was all before me, right?"

I replied with a soft "Yes."

"Then it's over today. All that stuff happened before you met me. I love you, and we can do *anything* we want, as long as we are together."

In that moment, most of my pain, worry, and guilt just melted away. For the first time in years, I finally felt *safe*.

Craig was the first person I ever really let know everything about me. That's not exactly the truth, since I don't even remember everything that I've done in my life. Someone could come up to me right now and claim that I wronged them terribly, and chances are they are probably right. I've said before, I was not a very good person. But I did share with Craig every story I could remember, every lie I told, every immoral thing I ever did. Allowing me, for the first time, to feel free.

This wonderful man brought me out of my fog. Embraced my heavy baggage and loved my daughter. He taught me that I was good enough to be myself, that if I had a skill at something I should show it. That I shouldn't hide things because I don't want to call attention to myself. That I should be bold and open. Granted, I might've taken that piece of advice a little bit further than he had intended, but without him I would be buried under more facades then I possibly could've handled.

He quickly thrived as a dad to Susan, and Susan took to him immediately. Craig was present for any extra activity in which she participated. He missed rock concerts, so he could be front and center for Susan's musical plays. He watched endless dance recitals, swim meets, volleyball games, and cheerleading competitions, just like any dad would do. He arranged for college and made sure she had everything that she needed. They created a bond so close that it sometimes made me upset, since those two will gang up on me all the time. They had inside jokes, to which I wasn't privy. They had a big laugh when a stranger would comment on their resemblance or how she "had" her dad's eyes, not realizing that they didn't share the same DNA. They would just giggle to each other, never correcting anybody, just letting the misconception stand.

Whenever I felt jealous at their closeness, I would check myself and realize that I had finally achieved one of my most improbable dreams. A normal life and a happy family.

After telling Craig my story about the Demon and his abuse, he suggested I take the address from the Christmas card, use the internet to find his phone number, and call to confront my abuser. Somehow, I found the strength and made the call. This became the first phone conversation I ever taped, six years prior to recording my mother's chats. I still have his tape, but to this day I cannot stand to listen to it.

During the call, he never admitted to doing anything wrong. He simply stated, "I drank a lot back then, I don't recall doing anything like that. That doesn't sound like me." Of course, I knew he was lying. If you got a call out of the blue from someone you hadn't heard from for years, and they accused you of molesting them, you would call them a liar, not hem and haw about what you can remember. Therefore, his vague answers and "woe is me," "I can't remember," statements were enough of an admission for me.

It was a cathartic moment for me. It allowed me to release a great deal of my anger and pain. The confrontation let me wrest control of my life away from him. I still feel the ripples of his violation, but they've been mitigated, and I have healed more than I ever thought possible.

With Craig's unconditional love and support, as well as my confrontation of my molester, I was able to begin my recovery process.

Lesson learned: What's your mountain? Own it. Climb it.

Medical Error

Although years of smoking, unhealthy eating, and genetics had taken their toll on my mother's heart, it was a medical mistake that ultimately slammed the final nail in her coffin.

My mom had her first heart attack on November 1, 2005. When she went to the hospital, they realized she needed a stent put in her artery. A stent is a metal or plastic tube that is inserted into an artery to help keep it open. She required it to help her heart to work more efficiently, obviously because the artery was clogged. Due to her large size, they had to position her on the table with her head far below her feet to accommodate the procedure. When they did so, her breathing slowed dangerously (basically because in that position, her weight was pressing down on her lungs), and therefore the doctor didn't feel comfortable giving her sedation medication, which could complicate the situation. They did give her a "twilight" injection, which helped her to relax without making her unconscious, but the operation was completed without any anesthesia at all.

The doctor came out and told us what happened, mentioning that she was awake during the procedure and that she was a trooper. We were greatly relieved to hear the surgery was a success, but the doctor was quick to warn us that she was not out of the woods yet.

After she was in recovery for several hours, they moved her to a room for observation. It was a normal hospital bedroom: drab, full of unfamiliar sounds, smelling slightly of ammonia and some other unidentified scent. But I was able to sleep semi-comfortably on the couch in her room while she rested, happy with the knowledge that she was doing better.

The next morning, we noticed that Mom was acting strangely. She seemed "out of it" and "loopy," her sleep was constantly disrupted, and when she tried to walk she looked like a newborn giraffe. Her nurses explained to us that she was probably having a hard time recovering from the twilight medication. We were doubtful that it would still affect her so long after the procedure but agreed to wait and watch for another hour.

However, Tracy and I started to notice something was seriously off. She had never behaved like this before, and by now, anything in her system would have been gone. Eventually the doctor made his rounds, and when he listened to our concerns, he asked, "Does she normally sleep a lot? Is she normally hard to wake up?" We answered him, "Yes, but not like this, not this long." The doctor left the room, seemingly concerned. I noticed him walk over to some of Mom's nurses and consult with them. I had no idea what he was asking for and no idea what he was doing. But now I *did* know something was not right, that was obvious.

I grasped Tracy's arm and told her to drive home. This was before smart phones became so common, and to do the research we needed required a desktop computer. Tracy lived 5 to 10 minutes away from the hospital, so it didn't take her long to get to her house. Within 15 minutes of leaving the hospital, she called me in a panic, shouting, "She's poisoning herself Kimmy! She's been a smoker for so long, and now her heart is working so much better, it's pumping more blood to her body, and her body can't handle the increase. She's probably what they call a 'CO_2-retainer.' Have them test her blood gases now!"

I hung up the phone and before I could make it back to the nurses' station, the nurse was walking into Mom's room to check on her. I asked the nurse to check Mom's CO_2 levels, explaining that she was a lifetime smoker, which might account for her strange behavior.

The nurse tersely told me she didn't need to run those tests.

"I see," I told her. I turned to face her straight on, lowering my voice to a menacing tone. "Well, that's quite a risk to take, because if anything happens to that woman, you can be sure that I will be suing you for malpractice."

The next thing I knew, Mom was being tested. I honestly don't know if it was my threat that got the ball rolling, or if the doctor noticed Mom wasn't her normal self and ordered the tests. I didn't care why it was happening, I just needed answers.

The next 30 minutes were a blur of nurses and doctors taking tests, trying to awaken her, waiting for results. When the test results came back the doctor came in and explained that she had in fact been poisoning herself. It seems that when someone's heart has worked at such a low capacity as Mom's did for so long, the body gets accustomed to the lower oxygen level. So, when her heart capacity was restored, she was receiving far more oxygen than usual, more than her lungs could process properly, which then resulted in CO_2 building up in her body. I'm sure there is a far more comprehensive and diagnostic description of the situation, but this is how it was explained to me.

To try to treat Mom for this condition, they started by putting her on a machine to possibly blow off the gases. However, when they tested her again, her CO_2 numbers had climbed even higher. This began a downward spiral, leading to another medical crisis.

They rushed her to the ICU and I quickly followed behind. The doctor stopped me at the glass sliding doors and asked me to leave, because they needed to stabilize her, and at this point they were very concerned. I turned to walk away, but then quickly twirled around to shout, "I love you, Mom!" Just before the doors closed, I glimpsed the medical staff intubating her. That's an image I wish I could scrub from my brain.

We waited for what seemed like forever before they allowed us to go back and see her. She was out of it for the next several days. Eventually, she came around and wanted to talk. Obviously being intubated makes talking difficult, so we brought in pens and paper, so she could write messages and let us know what she needed.

Her medical journey alone could probably fill another book, but suffice it to say, we had many ups and downs over the next three years, including her tracheostomy, which ultimately led to the creation of my precious tapes.

I'd like to offer some advice to everyone. Western medicine is amazing. Doctors and nurses have thankless jobs, sometimes. They work long hours and have many sleepless nights. But they are human, and humans do make mistakes. Be involved in your loved ones' care. Do research and learn what you need to know, ask questions when you can, and never feel timid about demanding answers from medical professionals. No one loves your family like you do, and no one will mourn them like you will, if they don't do their jobs properly.

I sometimes wonder if it would've been better if Tracy and I hadn't noticed that her body was polluting itself. If we hadn't, perhaps she just would've passed quietly in her sleep. Maybe that would have been far more humane for Mom than keeping her in agony for three years. However, I am selfishly glad that I had those three extra years with her.

Lesson learned: Ascertain. Ask. Act.

Memories That Speak

When Mom first became ill, and before any of us knew that she wouldn't be coming home to us, she said something to me that struck me like a right hook and forever changed my life.

I was sitting in her hospital room, chatting with her about her life and her family. She talked to me about her mom, my grandmother. I had only one memory of my grandmother, when I was about three years old. I remember laying with her in her bed while she was holding my younger sister, Mackenzie, who was only six months old at the time. Grandma was wearing a turban because she had lost her hair to cancer. She looked so frail. Six months following the events of that memory, Grandma was gone.

Mom explained to me what a close relationship she had with her mother, and how broken she became after Grandma's death. She went a bit crazy after her passing, hearing and seeing things that weren't there. She stopped taking care of Tracy, Mackenzie and myself for a while. In fact, she went to the doctor to have a brain scan to see if there was anything physically wrong with her. Nothing was found, and eventually she pulled herself together, but it took quite a bit of time, she said.

"You know what I miss most about my mom, Kimmy?" she asked. "I miss seeing her of course, but I miss hearing her voice even more. When someone dies, the memory of them lives on within you, but their voice is erased forever."

I was blown away. I sensed immediately the significance of her statement and decided right then that I would prevent such a loss from happening to me.

I left the hospital and rushed to a Radio Shack, where I bought a tape recorder that attached to the house phone. Whenever we answered the phone or made a call, it automatically recorded every conversation. It recorded all the mundane and unimportant things in a person's life: What time the car was going to be fixed and ready for pickup, what was for dinner, my husband calling to check in, Susan telling me she made it to her friend's house, and dozens of other routine chats with family and friends. The recordings were made with everyone's consent. They all understood that I would be recording my mom and that anytime they called my house, a tape was being made. Although these tapes became filled with commonplace stuff, they also gave me one of the greatest gifts I have ever been given: the gift of a memory that speaks. It's an audible recollection that can transport me through time. Her voice conveys me to what she was feeling, what she was thinking, what she was worried about, what provided her comfort. To listen to such memories helps me laugh at life and cry at the possibility of death. Even though the latter was hard to fathom, I'm glad I knew how she felt and what she wanted. How many memories would I have missed if I had waited even one more minute to begin taping?!

Why on Earth didn't I tell Tracy and Makenzie how to set up a tape recorder on their phones? I was so concerned with capturing my own memories with Mom that I didn't even consider that they might want to have their own saved memories. I have sincere regret that I didn't help them.

Since Mom was fitted with a tracheostomy, she couldn't talk to us. After five days of utter frustration, Mackenzie and I created an alphabet-board for her. When she had something to say, we would hold up the board and she would painstakingly spell out what she was trying to communicate. The method was agonizingly slow, but at least she could express herself. Following another five days of using this method, I mentioned what we were doing to my

Uncle Carl, and he showed up the next day with a surprise: a Leap Frog brand Leap's Phonics Library child's learning toy. It was like an old-fashioned Speak-n-Spell, but this device was a blue and yellow plastic pad with buttons on the front for the letters of the alphabet. Now, instead of pointing to a board, Mom could press the letters and the device would say the letters out loud, speeding up the communication process.

When I finally returned home after nine months of caring for Mom, she started to become extremely lonely. Family would visit, of course, but there would be long hours of every day where she was alone and wanted to talk to someone, but no one was there. She told me that the overnight isolation was more than she could handle.

"Oh, the nighttime is so lonely, Kimmy," she told me.

I could call her, naturally, but she wasn't able to speak, and the Leap Frog wasn't quite audible when she tried to use it over the phone. Eventually, we began using a sort of shorthand Morse code between us: a system of beeps and pulses using the number keypad on her phone. One for yes. Two for no. Three for either "I love you," or "I need something." Unlimited beeps if there was something wrong. It got to the point that our code was second-nature. I knew right away what she was saying, just from beeps.

I would call her up, and when she picked up the phone, I would cheerily say, "Hello, Wonderful," which was my nickname for her. She would just begin pushing buttons, and I would communicate with her by speaking normally.

The strange thing was, I never *heard* the beeps when we talked, I only heard her voice. To this day when I listen to the tapes, I hear her and not the mechanical tones she used when she couldn't talk.

At some point, that clever woman figured out a way to flex her throat muscles to deflate the balloon that was blocking air from passing her vocal cords. Since the air was now bypassing the trach, she was finally able to slowly communicate verbally. The hospital staff would be exasperated, refill the balloon, and stop her from talking again. But only for a short time, until she undid their work yet again. On the days when she could talk, which was most days because, let's face it, she was crazy-stubborn, her normal soft voice was replaced with a hoarse, forced-for-breath rasp that truly sounded nothing like her…except to me. My ears could fill in what my heart wanted to hear. And I recorded as much of it as I possibly could.

This went on for almost a year before she passed. The result was hundreds of hours of my mom's life story in her own words (or her own beeps, depending on the day).

As I mentioned in the Preface, to mark the tenth year of her passing, I gave myself the task of listening to those tapes and gathering the stories, laughter, and tears that I found there and collect them into a book that I intended to publish. The fact that you hold this book in your hands is a testament to the love and respect that I still hold for my dear mother.

Lesson learned: Yell your story.

The Bitch in "B"

In 2002, long before Mom fell ill, I had just moved in to Camp Lester military housing on Okinawa, Japan, due to Craig's Permanent Change of Station (PCS) to Kadena Air Base. We were assigned to a housing unit in a small, cinderblock four-plex, unit 6175-D. The building was painted tan, inside and out, with white tiled floors which created a God-awful echo, necessitating several rugs to help the acoustics. It was not very wide, perhaps 30 feet or so, but it was long and had a second story for the bedrooms, making it plenty big enough for the needs of our small family.

I had not yet met the neighbors in units A or B, but did meet my immediate next-door neighbor in C. I don't recall "C's" name, but I do remember she had two dogs. They were stocky, raucus beagles that ran amok in the neighborhood. I really wanted to complain to her, and normally I don't self-edit, but this was my first time living in military housing as an adult, and I didn't want to alienate myself to the neighbors right out of the gate.

I'll never forget the day I met the neighbor in B, Marquita Parkan. Anyone that knows anything about military life knows that a PCS move is stressful, exhausting, and downright overwhelming. After moving most of our possessions into the new house, I grabbed a glass of water and sat my ass down on the front stoop, defeated for the day. I sat there idly chatting with "C" when a sassy, short-haired brunette walked up to introduce herself.

Before she could say anything, "C" casually mentioned to her, "Your grass looks like it's growing, finally," or something along those lines.

The brunette displayed a supremely annoyed expression and replied curtly, "Well it would be if you'd keep your fucking dogs off of it!"

I was floored. I was not expecting this sort of interaction at all in my new neighborhood. Before I could recover, she leaned over and put her hand out to shake mine and said "Hi, I'm Marquita, the bitch in B!"

I quickly composed myself, smiled, and shook her hand before getting up to go inside. Once I made sure the door was secured behind me, I yelled for my husband to come downstairs, so I could express to him how much this "bitch" and I were *so* not going to get along.

"That lady is an asshole, babe, and there is *no* way we will ever be friends," I told him. Craig had no idea what the hell was going on, so he wisely mumbled something about being sorry that I had to deal with such a situation, then retreated to his man-cave.

In time, my prediction turned out to be the furthest thing from the truth. Marquita was my running partner (let's be honest, in my case, walking), my shopping buddy, my confidant, my 100-yen store companion, my craft teacher, my babysitter and my call-me-on-my-bullshit adviser. She's one of the few people who I never had to be "someone else" when I was around her. She got me like very few people could and loved me for *me*, flaws and all. Trust me, there are no shortage of flaws.

We did get into fights, though. Wow, we got into it! Knock-down screaming matches in our kitchens, or even on the sidewalk, always ending in two slammed front doors. Each time, I would march in and vent to Craig, vowing that *this* time, "…mark my words, I will NEVER speak to that woman again!" He would sagely nod, give me a hug, then turn over and continue to read his novel. It normally took about week, sometimes two, before one of us would call the other and ask, "I'm going to the store. Do you need anything?"

Just like that, all was forgiven.

Without this wonderfully quirky, profane, straight-shooting bitch in my life, my first years living in Japan would not have been so enriching and memorable.

Several years after we both left Okinawa and went our separate ways, we had the chance to get together again for Susan's birthday. I couldn't even recall which birthday it was, her fourteenth, I think. I just know that the band Fall Out Boy was coming to perform a concert in Oklahoma City's Ford Center Arena, and Susan was giddy about seeing them. I even managed to wait for *nine* hours in line with her, so we would be first in line when the band signed autographs at the Base Exchange. I nearly came to blows with some official who tried to escort a senior-ranking officer's children ahead of us in line. Susan met the band first.

By now my mom had been sick for about two years and I was looking forward to giving Susan a much-needed break to take her mind off her grandmother's illness. Craig was going to be deployed during the concert, and I needed a helper. I thought to myself, "Hey! Marquita could come out to help me chaperone ten teenage girls, and we can have a great time!" She agreed, and we finally had a wonderful excuse for a reunion.

Shortly after she arrived, we were hanging out in my bedroom, with Marquita propped up against my invisible headboard (I always *meant* to buy one), and I was laying across the base of the bed. We were talking about how good it was to finally see each other, how awesome it was to get our daughters together again, and what kind of mischief we could dream up.

At this point, the phone rang. I picked it up to the familiar sound of short and long beeps coming from the phone receiver.

"*Beep.*"

"Hi Mom, do you need help with something?"

"*Beep.*"

"Do you need Dad?"

"*Beep, Beep, Beep.*"

"I'll call him for you."

"*Beep.*"

"You're welcome, Mom."

"*Beep, beep, beep, beep, beep.*"

"Just sitting here with Marquita."

"*Beep, beep*"

"Yeah, from Okinawa."

"*BeepbeepBEEPbeep.*"

"Okay, I'll call Dad, Love you later, bye."

"*BEEP BEEP BEEP.*"

Mom had called looking for help in locating my dad because the nurses' station wasn't answering. There was no lapse in the conversation, no pauses while I tried to figure out what she was saying. She beeped and I just knew what she said. I hung up the phone turned back around to Marquita, who had obviously heard the conversation, looking shocked. Even across the bed, she was able to hear my mom's beeps over the phone.

"You always told me you talked to your mom like that, but until today I never really believed it, just thought you were exaggerating. Kim, that was the craziest thing I've ever seen. It's is so amazing and wonderful. How did you know what she was saying?" she asked.

"I don't know, I just do," I replied.

It was the very first time anyone outside of my

family had heard my mother and me communicating this way. It was such a pivotal moment for me, because I felt like someone finally understood my innate *need* to connect with my mother and the hurdles I was forced to leap to achieve that impulse.

For this reason, and for so many other factors that make up our private bond, the "Bitch in B" will always be someone special to me.

Lesson learned: First impressions only stick around until the second ones show up. Don't judge too quickly.

I Wouldn't Need Anything Else

It wasn't until my mid-twenties before I outgrew my self-destructive ways. Once I did, I wondered what it would've been like to live near to Mom after I had gotten my act together and became a functional adult.

Mom would also daydream about having me as a neighbor. After I had finished transcribing the first couple tapes, I noticed now frequently she mentioned it, and I began to realize how much it would've meant to her.

"How wonderful it would be if you were my neighbor," she said, and went on to describe her small domestic fantasy.

"We could wake up, take little Suzie Cute (her play on Susie Q) to school, and head out for coffee. Every now and then we would catch a movie or go grab lunch. Go get cookies and just laugh and talk." She spoke like she was dreaming of winning the lottery.

"If I had you as a neighbor, friend, and daughter,

Jesus! I wouldn't need anything else."

She didn't only mention this dream on the phone, she would talk to me about it when I was visiting as well. Every time she talked about it, she would have a little, sideways, mischievous smile, and would give me a little wink, as if to say, "I'm not gonna put that burden on you but, God, how I wish it was true."

My life with Craig, my husband and best friend, has afforded me the ability to travel around the world and meet new and exciting people. I love life with him and wouldn't change anything. However, it did take me further away from my family. It kept me from regular, morning, coffee chats, runs to the supermarket, and occasional dinner with Mom. How hard it must've been on her to not have her best friend close by. Even more than that, she missed out on having her "Suzie Cute" near her. She would recount to me on numerous occasions how difficult it was for her that Susan was not around every day. That Suzie was so much more than a grandbaby to her, that she helped raise her and her heart was broken when she left.

When listening to the tape, I can hear the deep sadness in her voice, but I also feel the deep love that is reflected in her words. How great is it to be loved that much? How lucky was I to be given to a mom like that?

You are my constant neighbor mom, because you are always in my heart. Although I don't drink coffee, I do regularly sit with you and chat.

Lesson learned: Life will never fill in all the pieces.

Twinkies and a Coke

Disclaimer: I'd like to take a moment to direct this comment to the fine folks at Hostess brand and Coca-Cola, and most especially to their lawyers. Twinkies are an amazingly delicious snack that I enjoy to this day. Coke is a wonderful beverage. Any described distress associated with said Twinkie or Coke products were due ENTIRELY to the lack of responsibility and forethought (in other words, stupidity) of the participants of this event.

Please don't sue me.

There are some stories in your life that just become personal legends. They are stories you end up telling almost everyone you meet, since it helps define who you are. One of my favorites is about my first brush with death, and it just so happens to involve Twinkies and Coca-Cola.

A couple of years before Mom got sick, I was visiting her, and we were bored. We sat in her house trying to dream up interesting things to do. By now, congestive heart failure was beginning to affect her health (though we didn't know it at the time) and she wasn't able to walk very far, which severely limited our options. Unable to come up with anything concrete, we just decided to get in the car and go for a ride, allowing fate to help us decide.

We drove around at random for about an hour, simply following the road and chatting about our lives and our dreams. Eventually, we noticed that we were about to pass a Walgreens and decided that a cold beverage would hit the spot. I told Mom to wait in the car and I would go in and get her a Coke, when she mentioned, "Hey, a snack would be nice, too."

"What do you want, Mom?" I asked.

"I don't know, surprise me," she replied. "Wait a minute. You know, I haven't had a Twinkie in forever!"

"Good idea! We can share a package of Twinkies," I suggested.

She scoffed. "Bullshit. You can't *share* Twinkies. Each one is, like, two bites of snack cake! I can eat a whole package in just four bites."

I grinned wickedly. "Four bites? Hmmmph. My ass! I can eat that package in *two* bites!"

She turned in her seat to look me in the face. Her expression had just lit up. "Oh, my gosh, Kimmy! Go get two packages of Twinkies and two Cokes…we're gonna have a Twinkie-eating contest!"

Oh yeah, this was going to be fun! I rushed into Walgreens, picked up two packages twinkies and two 12-ounce bottles of Coke, then quickly returned to the car.

I took out two packages of Twinkies, unwrapped them and placed them on the dashboard in front of Mom, then repeated the procedure for myself. We each opened our sodas and put them on the dashboard too, so they would be ready when we needed them.

Mom looked at me with a huge grin and counted down, "Ready, set, GO!"

I grabbed a Twinkie and shoved it into my mouth. Out of the corner of my eye, I saw Mom doing the same thing. I didn't even bother to chew, I just took the second one and shoved it right after the first, attempting to swallow both snacks whole, like I was a snake trying to swallow two yellow, cream-filled rodents.

This was about the point where I realized that I had made a huge mistake.

There was far too much of the product in my mouth, and I was not going to be able to swallow it without some sort of assistance, so I picked up the bottle of Coke and took a big swig in a futile attempt to wash down the Twinkies.

Some of you already have figured out what happened next.

For those of you who were not aware, mixing large amounts of carbonated soda with highly-sweetened, spongy snack cakes only makes them swell in an extremely quick manner. I was getting acquainted with this fact promptly, and found I had Twinkies lodged in my throat with no immediate clue as to how to remove them. Suddenly terrified, I looked over at Mom for help.

I saw that her eyes were bugging out of her head, looking at me for assistance. She had encountered the exact same problem.

Uh oh.

As our eyes locked, we each saw genuine fear welling up in the other person. Simultaneously, we swung our car doors open, leaned out over the door frame, and shoved our fingers in our mouths, scooping out soggy cake and cream filling as fast as we possibly could. It seemed like a full minute, but I suppose it was only several seconds later when I was able to excavate enough of the expanding Twinkies to reach my fingers to the back of my throat and dredge out what was lodged in my gullet.

Once I could finally take a breath, I spat out what was left in my mouth, sputtering and coughing to remove everything. At about this time, I noticed that Mom was coughing too, and I glanced over to make sure she didn't need any of my help. Fortunately, we both were able to recover on our own. After catching my breath, I put the car into reverse to drive us home.

As we backed out of the parking space, we saw the mess that we each had made. It looked like Twinkie the Kid and his buddies had gotten involved in a shoot-out in the Walgreens parking lot.

It was disgusting.

As we drove home, we talked about the disaster that could have been.

"Kimberly," Mom said, "could you imagine what the headlines would have said? *'Two Fat Women Die in Bizarre Twinkie Accident!'*"

We started choking again, but this time it was because we were laughing so hard. I was forced to pull to the side of the road and succumb to my laughter…great big, heaving guffaws that left my abs feeling like I had just done 500 sit-ups (which I have never done). We had trouble catching our breath and were lightheaded, but there were also tears of happiness for just being with each other and sharing such an outlandish experience.

Commonly, Mom would tell us that life "wasn't

worth the trip" for her, but after moments like that, I sure hope she changed her opinion, even if it was only a little.

As I was listening to the tapes of my recordings of Mom, I found the recording where we talked about this story, and what she told me made me beam with happiness and cry with sadness at the same time. I'm including a transcript of the tape here, but if you wish to hear the recording yourself, go to Youtube and search for "Loveyalaterbye".

Mom: Man, what the hell, you have gotten me into more shit…the Twinkies. [us laughing]

Kim: Two fat chicks die in a green SUV, in a Walgreens parking lot!

Mom: It was white and foaming, but until there is an autopsy, we can't tell you what it was.

Kim: Mom, let me ask you something. When you bit that and took a drink of that soda, when was the instant you realized "I shouldn't have done that!"?

Mom: As soon as I went to swallow.

Kim: When that stuff exploded in my mouth, you know when I had that Twinkie and…

Mom: It did, didn't it?

Kim: It did! I shoved that Twinkie down my throat, and then opened that soda, and thought that I would swallow that Twinkie whole. I took a drink of that soda, and it just exploded in my mouth! I couldn't feel anything in my throat.

Mom: I know.

Kim: And the whole time, all I'm thinking is, I'm going to die a fat chick, in a parking lot, with Twinkies running out of my mouth.

Mom: Yep.

Kim: And I shoved my fingers down my throat. You did too, huh?

Mom: Yep.

Kim: And we were outside, both of us, puking out the side car door. We came up at the same time crying. It was just hilarious!

Mom: I thought, what the fuck have I done? [Kim laughs] My daughter's killed me!

Kim: What made us do that, that day?

Mom: I think it was me.

Kim: I can't remem…

Mom: We were talking and I said, 'you know, I haven't had a Twinkie in years.'

Kim: Yeah, I was talking about the fried Twinkies at the fair. Yeah, and you said you hadn't had a Twinkie in a long time.

Mom: And we had to stop at Walgreens and you came out and you had Twinkies, and I think I said, 'man, that looks like two bites.' And you looked at me and said, 'well, I can do it in one.'

[Kim laughs] And I said, 'yeah,' and I watched you put that Twinkie, and that Twinkie was like the sword swallower. It disappeared, and then you went to take a drink while I'm getting it in my mouth, and I'm trying to hurry, 'cause you're making time. I get my soda, take a big swig, went to swallow, and that's when my pipes clogged up.

Kim: I was so scared, for real, Mom.

Mom: See, I didn't know you were in trouble.

Kim: I knew you were in trouble. I turned to look at you, and you looked at me, and your eyes were huge. I thought, 'oh shit! She's not going to be able to help me!'

Mom: Yeah, I pulled a wad of Twinkies out of my mouth…

Kim: [interjecting] Good times!

Mom: …that looked like a small ball of yarn I had to dig out.

Kim: I was terrified, Mom. Absolutely terrified.

Mom: That was absolute funny.

Kim: That was good times!

Mom: No, the best of times!

Lesson learned: Savor the sweetness of life. Don't try to shove everything in all at once.

Twinkie Addendum

There's a bit more to the Twinkie story, however.

One year after Mom died, I decided that as a tribute to her, I would buy a Twinkie and a Coke, and *safely* re-enact our favorite little memory. I only would take one bite of the cake, and one sip of the Coke, so the near-death peril was eliminated. Craig and Susan decided to join me in honoring Mom. A tradition was born. As time went on, other family members, and even good friends who have heard the story, have adopted our small ceremony.

A few years after the consumption of Twinkies and Coke became our family's annual ritual, we faced a serious impediment to its continuation.

In November 2012, just prior to our final move back to the States from Japan, Hostess announced that it was filing for bankruptcy and that it would be ceasing operations…including making Twinkies. Naturally, I reacted with panic, since I would no longer be able to continue my tradition after that year. Thus, began Twinkiequest 2012.

For two days, I scoured the island of Okinawa to track down every Twinkie I could find. They could only be purchased on military bases, but once the announcement was made, Twinkies were becoming scarce. I managed to talk to an on-base convenience store manager who was willing to part with two cases-worth of Twinkies, assuming I could come in immediately. I screeched into the parking lot in my trusty minivan, and nearly made a Kim-shaped hole in the door during my haste to arrive in time. But it paid off. I had them: $180-worth of Twinkies. I did some mental math and figured that with each of us eating one per year, this cache would last us around 15 to 20 years. Our ceremony was safe.

You should have seen the looks on the faces of the moving company packers when we told them to just pack up the boxes as-is.

The boxes made it safely with us to Colorado, and were stored in our cool basement, just waiting for our next ritual in August.

The day arrived, and we each took a Twinkie and a Coke, proceeding with equal parts gravity and joy as we celebrated Mom's life. Unfortunately, we noticed a problem right away. As we opened the cellophane wrappers and tried to pull out the snack cakes, they started to disintegrate. The consistency was wrong, as though a sponge was falling apart. They just weren't…right.

We couldn't believe it. Twinkies could go bad?? Surely this was a mistake. Everyone always joked that Twinkies could survive a nuclear apocalypse. Certainly, this wasn't happening!

But alas, it was true. $180-worth of Twinkies…and we had to throw them all out. Who knew?

Luckily for us, it had been announced just one month prior that another company would be buying Hostess and would continue production of their products. Boy, did we dodge a bullet. Mom's tribute was now safe.

Lesson learned: You can plan, but life has its own agenda.

August 24th, 2008, 9:15 a.m.

Throughout 2008, Craig and I had flown to Phoenix multiple times, usually with Susan in tow, each time due to doctors' warnings that, "…it looks like the time is quickly coming." So, near the end of August of that year, when we received yet another call telling us that Mom's demise was drawing near, we actually debated whether we should go or not, since we had only returned home three days prior, and felt that we should get Susan ready for school. We had made the journey so many times that it had almost become a family joke, even to mom. Ol' Linda was just yanking our chain again, maybe.

"We keep going there, and your Mom always pulls through, every single time," Craig argued.

"That's true," I countered, "but what if this really is the time, and I listen to you, and I miss saying goodbye? Could our marriage survive that?" It was my Aunt Jorja who had called us this time, the worry in her voice was unmistakable, and I was not willing to ignore the warning that was buzzing in my head.

He didn't say anything, just sighed deeply and nodded, resignedly. I had him by his shorties.

When we arrived in Phoenix, my Uncle Carl picked us up from the airport, and offered to take us to breakfast. I had never done this before, I had always previously gone straight from the airport to see my mom, but we were starving and exhausted from the quick turn-around, so we accepted his offer. After breakfast, we went directly to the nursing home where Mom was staying. Craig and I went to her room, but Carl decided to wait in the car.

By this point, she was kept rather sedated, so she was sleeping when we arrived. I went to the side of the bed and gently stroked her arm. She was breathing deeply and looked peaceful. To me, she did not look like someone who was on death's doorstep. I kept stroking her arm until she slowly drifted awake, opened her eyes, and looked at me with bafflement.

"Hi Mom!" I said cheerfully, "Surprise! I love you!"

The confusion deepened in her eyes and she managed to say something. "What the fuck are you doing here?" she demanded, softly. She knew that that we had just recently returned home to Oklahoma.

Craig, standing at the foot of her bed, could only chuckle. "You did it to us again, Linda! I think you just pull these stunts so that we'll visit, you!" Then he laughed to show her he was just joking around.

Mom's head swiveled towards Craig and she struggled to focus her eyes on who was speaking. Once she saw who it was, she turned back to me and asked, "What the fuck is *he* doing here?"

"We came to see you, Mom," I told her. "The doctors said we should come again." And you know I promised you'd never be alone when you die, I thought, but didn't say aloud. But by now she had closed her eyes again and drifted back into her chemically-assisted slumber.

I tried to wake her again. "We're going to Tracy's, Mom. I love you!" I kept nudging her for a response.

She opened one eye halfway, "Love ya, later," she mumbled, sleepily, then closed her eyes and dozed again.

We didn't know it at the time, but as far as we can tell, those were her last words.

We headed to Tracy's house and were able to grab a few hours-worth of sleep. I decided to spend the day with Mom, so I returned to the nursing home for the day, and Craig stayed at the house, so he could watch Susan and grab more rest.

Whenever I finished a visit with Mom at the nursing home, I tried to cheer her up with a dramatic exit.

I'd walk into the hall and turn in the opposite direction from the building entrance. Then I would pass her door with some sort of vaudeville dance step, flashing some jazz-hands and tipping my imaginary hat. Sometimes I'd perform disco moves, straight out of Saturday Night Fever. I once even tried to moonwalk. That was embarrassing. But each time they elicited a smile from Mom, which is what I always wanted. If she only managed a small grimace, I'd have to go back and try again with something different, until I received a laugh or grin from her.

As others of my family accompanied me on visits, they would at first look at me like I was nuts when they saw my "stage exit," but eventually they all started participating, too. I imagine the staff soon started to roll their eyes at the sight of three or four loony people in the hall, doing the running man, electric slide, or break-dancing past the door. Just prior to finally making my way to the exit, I would always pop my head back in the door one last time, point at her with a wink, and say, "Love ya later, Mom, bye!"

Upon leaving her room this time, just like every other, I made my dramatic exit. She never knew it, but I just had to do it.

I did not return to the house until very late that

night and ended up falling asleep on my sister's bed.

Early the next morning, on August 24th, I woke up sweating. I just had a feeling. I called the nursing home and spoke to one of the nurses, asking her to check on Mom. After a short wait, she returned to the phone and told me she thought it would be a good idea for me to come in right away.

I threw back the covers, got out of bed and went to the guest room where Craig was sleeping. I told him to get ready quickly, then went to wake up Susan, Tracy, and her family. Once we were in the car, I started calling family members and asked them to meet us at the nursing home.

When I saw her this time, I could tell that her time was short. Her face had a grey cast to it that I had never seen before. I sat next to her bed and stroked her arm and her hair, telling her how much she meant to me and how much she was loved.

Over the next hour, the family started trickling in by twos and threes. My dad, some of Mom's sisters, her nieces, most of the extended family who lived in town were able to show up. Eventually, the staff moved the additional bed out of the room to allow all of us to gather together in the same place around Mom.

Several conversations were going on all at once.

Many words could be used to describe my family, but "shy" and "meek" will never be among those descriptions. The stories started to be traded, and soon, despite the somber occasion that brought us all together, laughter began to fill the room. We spoke lovingly of all the good times we had had with Mom, and how much joy she had added to our lives. It's funny how you remember only the good experiences when someone dies.

After what seemed like hours, but was only probably 30-45 minutes, Craig, who was sitting off to the side and closely monitoring Mom, called to me to get my attention. "Kim! I think it's happening!"

I glanced down at Mom and saw that she had spat up just a bit onto her nightgown and looked like she was struggling to breathe. With almost military precision, a family member handed me some tissues to clean her face and clothing. They all then gathered around the bed and began to speak loving words to Mom.

"We love you Linda!"

"I will miss you!"

"You are loved, my sister!"

"I love you, sweetheart."

I held one of her hands, and Tracy held the other. I had Mackenzie on the phone, since she was still at home in Anchorage, because the next available flight wasn't until the next day. All the while we were leaning in near Mom's face, expressing our love for her. Less than a minute later, Tracy and I watched the life go out of her eyes. It happened so quickly, no one had time to alert Dad, who was down at the nurses' station. Craig signaled to a nurse, who was waiting just outside the door in the hallway, that she should come in and check on Mom. Dad followed her into the room. The nurse shouldered her way through the throng of family, felt for Mom's pulse, pulled on her stethoscope to listen for Mom's heartbeat, then nodded and said softly, "She's gone."

My relatives all started crying and holding on to each other, gathering comfort in the current closeness of the family. Craig held Susan as she sobbed. Tracy and I hovered over Mom with possessiveness, alternately happy the family was present to support each other, but also resenting their presence, since we craved privacy for our grief.

We stayed there in the room for another half-hour or so, until one of the staff members took me aside and told me that they needed to prepare Mom for transport. Mentally, I couldn't stand to stay in the room while they cleaned her, so Craig and Uncle Tim volunteered to stay in the room while the CNAs worked, to ensure Mom was treated with respect. Afterwards, we again stood by Mom's bedside until the transport arrived to take her to the mortuary.

When Mom was placed on the gurney and covered with a sheet, we all gathered outside next to the front door, waiting for her to be placed in the van. This is when my crazy and strange family stepped up to bring comic relief to the proceedings. Aunt Jorja was beside herself in grief and swore to herself that she would not leave my mom, insisting that she would travel with her the whole way to the funeral home. She told the driver of the van as much. The poor man tried to explain to her that he was not allowed to transport anyone but the deceased in the vehicle.

"That's okay, honey," she said, "I don't have to sit in the back with my sister, I'll sit up front with you."

The driver was flustered. "But ma'am," he told her, "there's a baby in the front with me."

"That baby can sit on my lap, sweetheart, I don't mind," Jorja replied. "I love babies." Later, she confided in me that she thought it was odd this man was doing his job while carting around his child.

The man was at a loss. He simply did not know how to explain to this woman that the baby in question was deceased, in a box. I took him off the hook, lightly grasped Jorja by the arm and moved her aside to explain the situation. Realization dawned on her face, and she reluctantly agreed to drive herself to the mortuary.

Secretly, I was almost pleased. Mom absolutely loved babies. She called them her "littles." I gained some solace from knowing that her last journey included riding with a little. I'd like to think that, if there is a heaven, she took that little peanut's hand, and led the way.

Lesson learned: Life is a heartbreaker.

Nobody Puts Momma in the Freezer

A few days before Mom's memorial, Aunt Debbie hosted a barbeque at her house, to continue the therapeutic connections that the family so desperately needed. More stories. More tears. More laughter.

I was sitting at a picnic table in the backyard when I was approached by Jorja, moms lifelong running mate, who I think might have also been using a prescription to help her cope. She continued to tell me about her special bond with my mom, and how close they were and how she was hoping she could continue that closeness. At first, I was confused, but then with dawning clarity, I realized what was coming. Everyone in the family knew that Jorja had a peculiar habit of keeping her dead pets in her garage freezer, since she couldn't bear to be parted from them. Surely, she wouldn't, would she?

"Honey, I have an important question for you."

No. No, this couldn't be happening.

"Kimmy, I can't stand the idea of Linda in that funeral home, or of having her in the ground, or burned up."

Nope, not happening. She couldn't possibly…

With a stone-cold sober expression on her face, she asked me, "Can we go down there, pick her up and keep her in my freezer?"

She did. I couldn't believe it.

"Jo, stop being silly!" I tried to play it off as her pulling my leg, though I knew she was being completely serious.

"I mean it! Let's go get her!"

At this point, everyone around us started laughing and trying to imagine out loud how we could pull off a heist from a funeral parlor to bring Mom's body to Jorja's house.

For ten days, the family was united in support. We shared food, laughs and tears…all of us trying to close the hole that we all felt in our hearts. We gathered photos of Mom…not an easy feat, since Mom *hated* to be photographed. We bought balloons and released them in her honor. I could swear that after the balloons were released, they spelled out "I L U." Others in my family claim they saw the same thing.

Preparing for the memorial service was one of the hardest things I've ever had to do. Even more so because I was never given time to mourn myself. I had to be the one that everyone else leaned upon.

Lesson learned: Buying a used freezer is a gamble.

Late to Her Own Funeral

The next few days are mostly a blur in my mind, and I am not at all certain of the sequence of events, but I have some very distinct memories during this time.

My mother was habitually late. She was never on time. I'm talking about the kind of late that if you wanted her to make it to a 7:00 event, you would tell her that it starts at 3:30. Even then, it was hit-or-miss whether she would be there. It was a bone of contention that eventually became a family joke. She would always excuse her tardiness by telling us that she simply always wanted to make a grand entrance.

During one of our conversations in the nursing home, I can distinctly remember talking to her about this.

"Mom, you're gonna be late for your own damn funeral," I told her.

"I will not!" she replied.

"I beg to differ!" I shot back.

"You don't know me! You don't know what I'll do!" This was one of her favorite comebacks.

"I'll bet you that I'm early for my funeral."

"Mom, you've never been early for anything a day in your life."

She really couldn't argue with that, and the conversation moved on to other topics.

Since Mom was something of a night-owl, we had decided that it would be appropriate to hold a nighttime funeral for her. I'm not saying she is a vampire but it wasn't very often you'd see Linda out in the daylight. Our intent was to give her a send-off she would have truly liked.

The morning of her funeral, August 28, 2008, I drove down to the mortuary to bring them the clothing she would be wearing along with her glasses. At the time, it struck me as rather odd why we were putting her glasses on her face, since she didn't need them anymore, but she always wore them and just didn't look like herself without them.

I completed some paperwork and was heading out of the office when a hearse drove up to the building. It was about 10 o'clock in the morning, but I didn't think there were any other funerals scheduled for that day, so I looked over to the funeral coordinator, Janice, and I asked her, "Is that my mom?

She initially looked a bit flustered and replied, "I, uh, no, uh, I don't know." At the same time, she kept walking, trying to guide me to my car.

I stopped and turned to look her in the eye. "Janice," I asked, "is that my mom?"

Janice avoided my gaze, looked down at her shoes in an embarrassed manner and said, "Yes, but she's not ready to be viewed yet."

"Oh, I don't need to see her, I just want to know if that *is* her."

"Yes. Yes, it is," she said.

I had to chuckle to myself. "Nicely played, Mom. Nicely played," I muttered.

Susan was with me, so I nudged her with my elbow and we did a little vaudeville-type shuffling dance past the hearse as we made our way to the car…just like we had whenever we exited her nursing home room. When we got to the front of the hearse, we stopped and yelled "WE LOVE YOU!"

We got into our car and looked at each other.

"Unreal, that woman was *Early* to her own damn funeral after all!" I shook my head in disbelief, then drove the car to Tracy's house to share the news.

After Mom's memorial, Tracy hosted a sort of wake at her house, and once again the family gathered together to share memories of Mom and lean on each other for support in our sorrow. Tracy was forced to see a doctor and to manage her heartache using prescription medication, therefore she was not exactly *there*. We all managed to get a few laughs watching her attempt to eat a tamale. She was a study of concentration, looking at the food in her hand with one eye open, staring intently, bringing the tamale up for a bite with her mouth open, but missing it by several inches. She only managed to chew air, but it must have been good air because she seemed quite happy with her meal.

I went outside to find many of my aunts smoking around a table, and Craig had joined them, puffing away. I was horrified. He *never* smokes and knows how much I hate it. Hell, *he* hates it, but I guess he was just very stressed at the time. I chewed his head off right there in front of everyone, accusing him of insensitivity by partaking of the same vice that played such a part in killing Mom. Guiltily, he stubbed out the cigarette and apologized. I realized how unfair I was being and apologized right back.

Soon thereafter, someone noticed that a lightning storm was moving in over the city. The sky lit up with nearly continuous lightning bouncing from cloud to cloud. The thunder was a continuous rumble. My entire family stood on the back porch, looking at the sky with tears in their eyes, murmuring that it was like Linda was giving us some sort of sign.

That she was storming her way into heaven, because she was more than happy to escape the hell of that hospital bed.

Lesson learned: Giggling eclipses grief.

I Should've Scratched More

When we lose someone close to us, we realize that there were dozens of little things that we could've done to make their life easier while they were with us. Favors that might seem small or insignificant to us make a huge impact to our loved one, especially when it's something they aren't able to accomplish on their own.

While preparing this book, I reviewed not only hundreds of hours of recordings, but also dozens of sheets of notebook paper that Mom would use to write on before she learned to talk around the trach. If I was out of the room because I was grabbing some food or getting some rest, Mom would jot down things she wanted to say or talk about when I returned. Frequently, it was quite difficult for me to read, since Mom was still learning to use her hands again, so the hieroglyphics she produced were usually hard to decipher. It generally looked like a child's handwriting.

One of the common requests I found on these old

messages were appeals for me to scratch her. I found several of these. Practically one or more on every single sheet.

I recalled that she was almost always asking me to scratch her. Her back, arms, legs, butt, even her scalp. Her mobility was gone by then, and she couldn't reach anywhere that was irritating her. I remember being exasperated often by the repeated requests, and sometimes I would scratch her, well, less-than lovingly. She would have me scratch her somewhere, which I did, and just after I was done and had sat down, she would claim to itch again and ask for more scratching. Once in a while, frustrated I would stand up, walk to her bedside, find the offending patch of skin, and just keep scratching at it trying to somehow prevent any future itching. Naturally, this harmed Mom more than it helped her. I was irritated, and I took it out on her, which I never should have done.

Years after she was gone, I was sitting in my house and I managed to get an itch on the very center of my back. The place where one simply cannot reach. One either needs a handheld back-scratcher or assistance from another person. Craig wasn't home, so it was up to me. I tried everything I could think of to stop the itching. First, I took off my shirt and used it like you would a towel after a shower, trying to scrub my back. Once that didn't work, I tried using my bra, hoping the coarseness of the embroidery would suffice to eliminate my agony. Still no luck. Next, I tried rubbing up and down on a door jamb like a bear using a tree in the woods. Dammit! Nothing was working!

At that moment, I suddenly had an image of Mom, reclining in bed, pumped full of medicine that created incessant itching, and tears started to well up in my eyes. Even further, I imagined that it wasn't necessarily the itch itself that was the torture for her, but a constant reminder that if she had something that needed to be tended to, sometimes she had no one she could count on. Whenever she had an itch without someone there, she had to lie there in anguish, knowing that she wasn't in her home, that she didn't have her husband with her, that she wasn't comfortable. In fact, maybe the itch became completely secondary to the fact that she didn't have anyone there for her when she needed them. That she was so totally and utterly *alone*.

When we all went home for the night, went to our jobs, and just lived outside of the walls that she was trapped within, the emptiness that had become her now-normal life was only magnified by my resentment of a simple kindness that she requested of me.

This realization awoke a new mindset within me. Ever since that moment, I have strived to separate myself from the "you scratch my back and I'll scratch yours" mentality, and instead foster a mentality of, "here, let me scratch that for you."

I wish I had scratched Mom more.

Lesson learned: I should've scratched more.

My Promise

One of the more painful things that Mom told me was, "It wasn't worth the trip for me. You should put that on my headstone." She said this often. In my mind, she was trying to explain that after she was born, she had such a painful, unhappy existence on Earth, that it wasn't worth it for her to have come.

Mom always had one request of me. Usually, she would make me promise that I would comply with the appeal before she even told me what the request was. Normally, I had to agree just to get her to continue with the conversation.

"It's really important that you promise, because I mean it, Kimmy," she cautioned.

"Okay, Mom, what is it?" I asked.

She leaned forward and looked at me with wide-open, serious eyes. "You listen to me, I'm not joking. When I die I want you to put on my marker, 'It wasn't worth the trip for me.'"

Holy hell, that was a powerful statement.

"What do you mean it wasn't worth the trip for

you, Mom?" I was flabbergasted.

"Kimmy, aside from your dad, you girls and those grandbabies, just like Dorothy said to the Wizard of Oz, there wasn't anything in that bag for me. I don't want you to get me wrong, I love my life with you guys, but that's all I ever really had."

I knew right then that there was *no* way I was keeping that promise. Surely such a caring, funny, loving, and bigger-than-life soul needed something more profound than that. In the end, what we did was not much better than what she asked for. We gave her was a simple marker, accompanied by a carved image of a cardinal, that says:

IN LOVING
MEMORY
LINDA UPCHURCH
APRIL 24, 1951
AUGUST 24, 2008.

At the time, I was too numb to think of anything else, but I was savvy enough to know that I would be breaking my promise to her.

It looks like I might have a grave marker to change. I'll do it mom, maybe, but if I do, I don't have to like it.

Lesson learned: Some promises are meant to be kept.

Her Promise

I, too, had a promise that I asked my mom to keep. Ever since she was young, Mom believed that she could see spirits. She didn't think they were harmful ghosts or poltergeists, nothing like that. She felt that she only saw souls that were lost, and that every so now and then they would show themselves to her.

As I got older, she shared stories with me, such as the time in military housing she met a young boy named Billy. Billy was kind of an odd duck. I mean, he was see-through, so that was alarming. She said he was mischievous and just a little bit naughty, but overall a good kid.

Then she told me about the time that she saw young ballerina girl, maybe four- or five-years-old in her bedroom holding a music box.

Both of those situations would be a big bag of nopes for me. I would leave the room, the house, the city. And not come back.

The story that she shared the most, though, was that of her mother. My mom said it was the middle of the night and she completely woke up from a dead sleep. She wasn't groggy or tired. Also, she had perfect vision, which was weird because she normally wore eyeglasses as thick as Coke bottles. She sat straight up and saw her mom sitting on the edge of the bed. Her mom softly said to her, "it will be all right," and disappeared.

One time, when she was retelling that story, I made her promise not to come back and haunt me. I told her that I loved her more than life itself, but my fragile brain just wouldn't be able to cope if I saw a semi-transparent Linda floating around.

These days, it's a promise I wish she had broken. Transparent or not, her presence would soothe me.

Lesson learned: Some promises are meant to be broken.

LYLB

Mom and I had developed a unique phrase that we used whenever we said goodbye. Commonly, we used it when we were hanging up a phone conversation. Initially, of course, we simply said, "I love you. Talk to you later." Eventually, Mom morphed that into a simpler, "Love you, later." Mom never liked to say, "goodbye." I would usually be the last one off the phone and I would shoot a quick, "Love you, later, bye," to her. Of course, ultimately it became quicker and quicker until it started sounding like, "Luvyalater, bye." I really don't think she appreciated the "bye" part that I included, because every now and then she would hastily insert one last "later" before we disconnected.

The busy days leading up to Mom's funeral were filled with so many details to arrange, I was not left with much time to lament. I was handling most of the details that survivors are required to supervise. In addition, I was loving, helping, protecting, and comforting my sisters. They needed me a great deal, and truth be told, I *needed* them to need me. Ironically, I don't think I would've made it through that time if they had held it together more.

There is something I wish I had said at her funeral, but I didn't get my chance. Since I was so caught up in the sadness of the event, responsible for ensuring that my little sister was okay, confirming that my dad was holding it together, and making certain that my older sister, under the influence of prescription medicine, was not lighting the chapel on fire, I just didn't articulate the message that I so desperately wanted to convey.

Since I never got the chance to say it at your funeral, Mom, I'll say it right here: I love you, Mom. I hope I'll see you later, and goodbye for now.

Lesson learned: Don't get so caught up with helping other people that you forget to take care of yourself.

Final Thoughts

When I set out to write this book, my main goal was to disprove my mom's theory that her life "…wasn't worth the trip for [her]." I tried everything in my power to rummage through the multiple sad moments in my tapes to unearth her happier times. There just weren't very many to be realized.

My mom had an innate ability to make me ugly-laugh. Although I miss that, and her great stories, I believe now she used her humor to hide her truth: she was riddled with anxiety and severely depressed. It was probably something I have always known, but never fully understood.

She let life pass her by, always waiting for the perfect moment, for when she wasn't afraid, nervous, or dispirited. There were things she wanted to do in life that were left unaccomplished. Places to be travelled that were still too far away, and people she wanted to love and visit that were just out of arms' reach.

I know it wasn't an easy ride, but thanks for making the trip, Mom. You've taught me to make *my* trip worth it!

As a direct consequence of writing this book, I've decided that I will no longer wait for tomorrow. I'm not waiting perfect, I'm not waiting for skinny, and I'm no longer going to be scared to live because I might die. It's time to get drunk on life!

Anxiety can suck it!

Life is screaming at me from the proverbial pool, kicking back, laying on a float in the water, sipping a margarita, "Come on in! The waters fine!"

And I'm gonna jump in, feet first! CANNON-BALL!

To Be Continued…

Lesson learned: Give yourself more than 2 ½ weeks to write an entire book!

Made in the USA
San Bernardino, CA
17 August 2018